Down

Down

the

Rabbit

Hole

Holly **Crawford**

ISBN-13: 978-0985246112
ISBN-10: 0985246111

Lokke Press
New York

CONTENTS

ACKNOWLEDGMENTS

I would like to thank Christine Palma, Jennifer Ashton, Bob Holman, Nico Vassilakis, Fred Dewey, Marjorie Perloff and my husband George Crawford for their help and encouragement with this work.

PREFACE

This book the "poems" of several small chapbooks
that I printed and gave to several people while my
husband was teaching at Stanford in the 1990s.
These chapbooks were available for several years
at Printed Matter's Soho space in NYC. They did
not gather dust on the shelf. When they moved to
smaller location in Chelsea they returned a couple
and sent a royalty check. Thank you. Some addi-
tional found punctuation poems are published in
Proliferation #5 edited by Mary Berger and Chris
Vitiello and The Last Vispo Anthology edited by
Nico Vassilakis and Crag Hill. Some of these poems
have never been published before. I find the his-
tory of punctuation to be very interesting. It keeps
evolving. I have given short talks on the history of
punctuation with the performances. The perfor-
mances have, to date been, on the radio and differ-
ent venues from Beyond Baroque's text festival,
the Bowery Poetry Club, Live in the Limo in NYC,
Melbourne International Arts Festival & the Lake-
side Theatre at the University of Essex, UK. The
little chapbooks that are Xerox copies on 8 ½" x 11
recycled grey paper folded in half and held togeth-
er with shoe string and silk chord, whatever was
available. These found visual poems are recycles
and reconstructed. They imply a narrative that is
missing or needs to be filled in and was with the per-
formances of these pieces. Now I have brought them
all together under the title Down the Rabbit Hole.
-Holly Crawford, July 2012

INTRODUCTION

Bringing the World into the Word:
Punctuation and Fracture Poems by Holly Crawford

One of the best known works by the late Italian
conceptual artist Alighiero e Boetti is a very large
drawing from 1973 called Bringing the World into
the World. It consists entirely of punctuation –
actually, only the commas – derived from an
invisible text. The commas, recurring at
irregular intervals, define the drawing, other-
wise a sprawling field of blue ballpoint-pen ink
marks, as a text. It is also a score, perhaps,
mapping time across space; but it is definitely a
text, its only cogent images associated specifical-
ly with linguistic notation. In this manner, Boetti
poeticized a trope already fairly widespread among
concept artists and concrete and visual poets (not
least among the Italian avant garde); while most
of his contemporaries were seeking to squeeze
the romantic and the sensual out of their verbal-
visual structures, Boetti sought to re-capture and
re-valorize such lyricism – in effect, celebrating
the bones of language as language, and as image.

The concrete poems Holly Crawford realized in
the later 1990s and early 2000s ordinate and
deracinate extant texts; but, in doing so, they, like
Boetti's World, expose a sensuality in textuality, a

meta-sense in the texts of others, and a visual charge – constant but not consistent – coursing throughout standard typography. Crawford subjects discursive essays (by, among others, Clement Greenberg and Rosamond Purcell) to dissolution and reassembly according to methods of her invention and adapted from others'; and, more broadly, she subjects writings of various kinds, prosaic and poetic, by various authors to reconstitution and revelation.

Crawford's reassemblies and revelations do not illumine their source texts so much as illumine the universe of textual comprehension into which all those source texts – and all texts – emerge. In effect, she finds her "meaning" in the nebula of possibilities ringing, in this case, the galaxy of English. Crawford drains her source texts of their narrative or polemic, deriving energy instead from the texts' drive towards meaningfulness. What remains on the page after Crawford renders the original texts is a derivation that tastes but does not look like its sources – not least because the texts have taken on a graphic presence that transcends language without entirely leaving it. Whether the words have been reordered or removed, what sits on paper signals us as much from the world of, say, dance or cave painting or microphysics as it does from the world of language. In certain of the poem-derived pieces one does sense an oblique meta-commentary on the tenor of the particular poetic expressions ("...the Romantics as full of question marks and exclamation marks," Crawford has noted, observing also that "punctuation became less important in the very early 20th century... Maybe [it was] considered just excess ornament...”). But the works ultimately stand alone, ghostly – or, more to the point, skeletal – reconfigurations, and thus reconsiderations, of the original.

Holly Crawford thus continues the project of liberation – bringing the word into the world, to paraphrase Boetti – to which so many great artists of the modern era have contributed. But she is careful not simply to set the word free into the world (as Boetti’s countryman F. T. Marinetti would have it), but to reverse the process as well, to invest the word with the world, to bring the world into the word, to liberate even the muted voices of punctuation and diacritical marks so that they sizzle with nascent expression. Pulled from texts of great weight and portent, Crawford’s pages jump with life.

Peter Frank
Los Angeles
September 2012

Hollow

Dog

words from Rosamond W. Purcell

Some of the allusions of dog(s), in *dog days* and *Hollow Dogs* [1] are to the actual dog, the cultural guardians as guard dogs, dogs as in "kitsch" culture, the process is dogged, and the process was derived and was executed in August. *Hollow Dogs* is the remnants and the space of the words and punctuation, of three paragraphs of an article by Rosamond Purcell.[2]

Holly Crawford
November 1995

---

1 One allusion is to *Hollow Men* by T.S. Elliot.
2 Her work, that was presented in the article, deals with the physical rearrangement of objects in museum display cases.

,

dog   died
during

•   •   •

display

'   '

'

hound

different

historical

•

,

-

,

:

dog.

Dog

,

hot death,

-

hole.

,

death

,
•

home hole.

Hollow

Dogs (   )

,

,

heads

domestic dogs

,

. dogs

,

,

dogs, Dutch
dogs

have

hides

.

dog

,

•

,

,

Dutch dogs,

,

human

,

.

have

—

•

,

dog
dig

,

dog

have

?

Negative Dog1

In 1990, the artist Allan Cullum poured plaster into
a rubber cavity made from a cast made from mold left by
a dog that died during the eruption of Vesuvius in A.D.
79. On display at the Boston Museum of Fine Arts as
part of an exhibition of contemporary art entitled 'La-
bels', three of four identical third-generation copies of the
hound were shown in different orientations expressive of
an infinitely renewable historical moment. While admir-
ing the resourcefulness of the artist and the postmodern-
ist, mass-market purposefulness of the enterprise, I missed
the authentic object: the empty shell of the actual dog.

The Pompeii Dog Replicas take the shape of an ani-
mal who was eventually metamorphosed, after a very hot
death, from an organic creature into a canine-shaped hole.
It seems to me that it is this original cavity, evidence of
death from volcanic gas and ash, which best represents the
event. I wish there were a method for bring home a hole.

Hollow Dogs (Fig 5) shows stiffened, skull-less heads
of baying domestic dogs who came from the countryside
in Holland around the time of World War II, and whose re-
mains were collected by van Heurn. The dogs were used,
it has been said, as food by starving citizens under siege.
Unlike McCullum's dogs, the Dutch dogs have kept their
hides but almost lost their shape. There is only one dog from
Pompeii, and even as an artifact he is beautifully refined
and undeniably valuable. After all, he represents a cata-
clysmic natural event in antiquity, whereas the Dutch dogs,
of which there are many symbolize a calamity caused, as

1 Rosamond W. Purcell, "The Game of the Name", *Art Bulletin*,
June 1995, volume 77, number 2, pages 180-185. The above
quote is from the section called "Negative Dog", pages 182-183.

usual by human beings, just yesterday.

Fossils are organic creatures or plants whose soft parts have been replaced by stone -they are casts of animals. So, if you were to place the cavity of the dog in mud and silt and dig it up again ten of thousands years from now, there would probably be a genuine stone dog inside the shell where the soft parts once were.

But who would have the time?

dog days

a process poem

words by Clement Greenberg

dog days is a recycled-process poem. It is constructed solely of the words in Clement Greenberg's article "Avant-Garde and Kitsch"[1] Severaldifferent processes[2] were utilized in the construction of this work. Methodical processes creating new forms. But not necessarily rational. No new words. There are many other methods available for selecting the words used here. I didn't play with different methods until a "right" one was found. There are perceived patterns and meanings. New meanings? No meaning? Process is the "thing" in art, science, law and other fields. The processes used were time consuming and tedious. Time and repetition, what do they add to the meaning? Does process and repetition create beauty, art, truth, law, or justice? Does form create beauty, art, truth, law, or justice? Does process have meaning? Does it create meaning? Does it reveal meaning? Or does form have meaning? Create meaning? Or reveal meaning? What "meaning"? These are some of the aesthetic issues which are addressed here.

Holly Crawford
August 1994

---

1 Greenberg, Clement. *Art and Culture, Critical Essays.* Boston, 1961.
2 See technical appendix.

A

a, a, a
a
 a

a
 a

a

above addition,
aesthetic all,
aesthetics age
an,
and
  an alley
and, and,...and...,

 And

an answer appears

ARE?

As, as, as avant-garde.
Between Braque and...
brought by,
by, by, by, by, by, by civilization, closely.

Connection?

Contents cover culture.

32

Culture?
Culture a different disparity.
Cultural dispariy does?
Does each, Eddie, enable and end
enlightening Eliot?

T.S. Eliot enough,
entirely.

Evening.
Examine experience,
experience exists,
fact.

Fact for frame.
Four generalized and
granted, the guest has been here. And
hitherto historical.

However, in, in, in, in
indicate the individual, investigation
involves,

Is it? is it kitsch? is large, is light,
Is Me?

Met more,
more, more,
more natural, necessary. New?
Not.

Of, of, of, of, of,
Of one or, order originality. Ostensibly
other.
Or order other

on Our painting.

Pan part and parts particular, perhaps.
perspective,
place
and poem.
Poem posed post
produces products, questions.

Question, relation,
relationship the same,
same Saturday seems same. Simultaneously
single.

Situate society.
Social somethings, song specific and such.
Such taken takes that and this.

Than and than...
That to, to that. ,....
 To the, the , the , the , the , the , the, the the
the , the , the,
the,
 things.
To them, to their, to that, to this
tin tradition.

Takes things, two
 to Us

What will? Which?
Which?
 Within.

I

a a a a a a abandoned absolute accidents
   aesthetics
   air
 Alexandrians all, all alone
 already although
 always and
and art,
art artists attitudes audiences, all, an
 and and and as and and art
  art are Aristotelian and Aristotle
Aristotle as and and and

Acquire, avant-garde be be be

be, be be becoming begins
belongs, Best.
Bohemia, bourgeois...Brancusi but,
but
But by

Can,
cannot,
CASE, centered

Century character, chief: circulation
coincided communication,
 compose contemporary
continue, constraint
contains

courage, crane, criticism, cultivated culture
culture deceived

different, difficult, even every,

every exclusion, expression
expression factors far
 far fifth
 formalism, forms, formulation
fourth

function general
God gone

Greek has
have,
have he
 here
his Hofmann, however imitated
imitates, imitating,
 imitation in in in in in in in

 independent into inside invokes it it it it
its
 itself, itself itself, itself is
is is Klee
kind,
 large, life long lectures
makes masters

means, means medium
modernist more
more
much music natural

near necessity needed
new not
novel of, of of of of of of of of of
36

on,
 once only
 or, or or or or
or originally
others,
 our out, outside own
own Plato,
 poetic poets preoccupation
 politics, process
process produced possible Procrustean

Quite reactionary
reference remark, remarks represent
response,
revolutionary, Rimbaud ruling
 sculpture

search,
seem
shown signa
 society , society soon
spaces
 starving state
stem
  still
struggle
symbols
than, that, that that that that that
the the the the the the the the the the the
the the the
the their, themselves
there, these, this this this this this
 timid true,
truth to
to to to to to to to to to to untouched

Up US

values was
was where
which, which with words
words work, worthy

would

                                    II

Where,

where

where, where

avant-garde?

                                    III

 of...
 paid in
simply
 becomes...

returning

38

IV

should as the train,
the find
the kitsch,
was high comprehension

w e
cultures
ballads gone
literature symbols
energy produce
former slave-owning
possess in Italy
is kitsch

level
they
  bring this culture,
a, to, with the, of and are
is kitsch

contact, to there
isolation
ask this, the a
at Kulturbolschewimus
of being politicians, the of
way
necessary, more circumstances
Germany, Stalin, capitalism
benevolent
than its elite served

administration

them,
into
 not coming
own culture
industry
whose made other, today
saw

culture

Appendix: technical processes

These are the processes used to deconstruct Greenberg's essay and construct the poem.

Clement Greenberg's essay consists of an introduction and four parts. A different process was used on each part. The parts of the essay correspond to the parts of the poem.

Introduction: All 225 words form his introduction were employed in the introduction of this poem. These words were, for the most part, alphabetized.

Part I: The instrument used to select the words in part I, was a pack of shuffled playing cards. The cards were numbered 1, ace through king, thirteen. The cards were then turned over one at a time. If a king was turned over I would count thirteen words from the last word selected. This process was then repeated. The ascertained words were then alphabetized.

Part II: The words in part II were selected from the words that corresponded to the respective Fibonacci numbers. The series is, 1, 1, 2, 3, 5, 8, 13, 21, 34, 55, ... This process was then repeated until the words were reduced to their minimum set. The string of words became shorter but did not disappear.

Part III: Every eleventh word in part III of the essay. The process of selecting every eleventh word was then repeated. Eleven was selected by a role of the dice. The words remaining are presented in order.

Part IV: The words from part IV were selected using a table of irregular primitive (prime) numbers, 37-1367. This process was then repeated using all the primitive numbers until there was only one primitive number-word. That word was "cultures."

the
bone

punctuation by Clement Greenberg

the bone

the bone is a long poem consisting of five punctuation poems, five punctuation "footnote" poems and a punctuation P.S. It is an exploration in form, structure and connections. The process removed all but the ultimate and underlying formal structure.

A review by Eliot Weinberger in *Sulfur 37* reported that the editor of one poetry anthology had "normalized" Emily Dickson's punctuation. Poems are more than words. Everyone's structures are different, but sometimes they're thrown to the dogs.

The poem *Hollow Dog* that preceded this work is not part of the Greenberg series. It was derived from an article by Rosamond W. Purcell. She rearranges museum displays to reveal new meanings. *Hollow Dog* was also a rearrangement.

Directional notes for a performance are:

Parenthesis and brackets, question mark and period may be read by the same people.

The prologue and P.S. should be read in unison by the group.

Footnotes may or may not be read aloud. It is at the discretion of the performers. When they are read, they should be whispered.

Holly Crawford

May, 1997

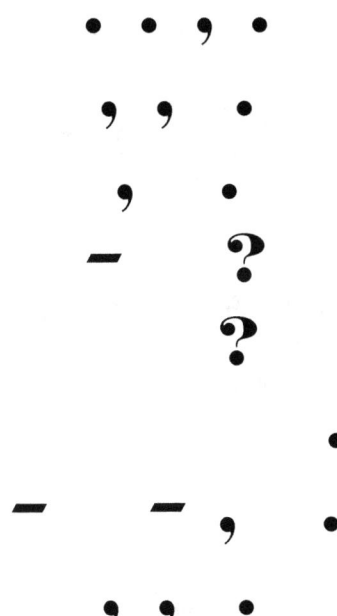

I.

, , , , •

•

, , , , •

, , , •

, • , , , , •

— — •

, : — •

— , , — •

, , •

, , " " , •

, , , •

, , — — , — •

48

, — — .

, , " " .

, •

, ' , •

(, , — —, ,— .)

— " ", .

, " " .

— " ", .

, — .

" ' " " ", .

— " " "" — , .

— , , — — ; , , , .

.

" , " .

, .

, — " " — .

" . "

, .

" , " , , .

, " . .

; , , .

: . ।

I.

,,‾,,.

,‾,‾‾‾ ‾.

,.

,,,.

,,: ",,."

,.

,,,‾ .

‾.

, , , , , , •

, , , , ⌐ , •

, , , , , , , " " , •

, , , •

, , ⌐ •

, , " " " • "

⌐ •

—, ' , ' , , , , • [2,3]

2.

, , •

, • " " •

, •

3.

‘ .

‒ ‒ ‒ .

; ; .

: , .

,, ' .

.

" , " " , " " " .

,, ‒ .

.

54

II.

,   •

— , : : , , , , , , , , , • , •

•

•

•

,,,,•

•

, ,   ',,•

‾,',•

,,,‾,•

,••,,,,•

, ˉ , •

•

•

•

, •

•

˗ .

,,,,, •

,,,,,, •

,, •

, •

, •

" ,"
, " •

,• , ,
" " •

, " ",•

‘ — , •

, •

, , , , •

, •

, , •

— •

, , , , •

, , , , , , •

, , ?

, , ; ?

, , •

62

, .
– ,, –’:
“… .”
: “ (), ‘ ?

, (‘:),
‘ ‘ ‘ .’”

,⁻,.

,.

,.

,,,,.

,,⁻ ,⁻ .

, " " .

,,.

.

, ; ⁻ ⁻ ; .

, .

,,, .

,,.

64

,, ‾ ,, •

,, , •

— ' , — , •

•

' •

— •

, ' — ; : — •

' — , — ,, •

— — •

— — : " •"

•

, :

,, •

.

,, •

,,,, •

, ⁻ ,,,, •

⁻ , •

, •

'   , •

" "   •

,, " " , '   •

, •

, •

, • 4

66

4.

, ?

III.

,,•

; – –   •

,   " "   " "   ,,,,•

– – –   •

, , •

, •

; •

, , •

,   •

. ▬ .

, .

, , .

, .

, , .

, " " .

, , , , ' ▬ , ▬ , ▬ ▬ , .

, , , ' ▬ .

▬ , , , .

" " , .

, , , •

•

, •

•

, , •

•

•

, ⁻ , •

⁻⁻ , , •

• ' , , ⁻ •

IV.

,, ,,　　',,　–　•

•

–　–　,, ,,　•

,, ,,　"　　•,,

,,　•

•

,, ,,　•　[5]

5.

– .

, – , ‘ : ,, .

, – ,, .

,, “,” – , .

, – , .

.

– .

– – .

‾,.

‾,,‾,,.

•

— — ‾, •

‾,•

(‒.)

,,‾,,, " , " , •

" " •

‾, •

, ⎯ , , •

⎯ , , ⎯ ⎯ •

, , , ⎯ ⎯ •

⎯ , , , ' •

⁏ , , ⎯ ⎯ ⁏ , , ⎯ •

•

•

, ⁏ •

74

,,•

—— — ,,▀•

,,•

▀ •

——•

•

——, ;•

•

; •

" • "

,, •,, •

•

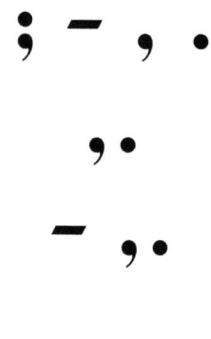

P.S.

; ‘ .
‘ .
.
[.]

In order of appearance:

dot   .

comma   ,

period .

dash -

question mark ?

hyphen -

colon :

quotation marks " "

apostrophe '

parenthesis ( )

semi-colon ;

bracket [ ]

dog...
praised
his fleas

dog...
praised his fleas is the third part of a three-part work
based on elements from Clement Greenberg's 1939
article, "Avant-Garde and Kitsch." All three parts have
utilized some aspect- words,
punctuation, and the
negative space- in his article.
dog... praised his fleas is based on the space between the
words, which I have
reduced to its numerical
values.

Holly Crawford,
May 2000-October 2001

One
hundred
and
fifty-
two,
seventy
-five.

One
hundred and
seventy-eight, two
hundred and
thirteen, one
hundred and fifty-
six, one hundred
and eighty, ninety-
eight, two hundred
and eighteen, two
hundred and sixty-
nine, one hundred
and forty-nine, one
hundred and
ninety-seven,
ninety-six, thirty-
nine.

Ninety-
five,
twenty-
six. one
hundred
and
two,
one
hundred
and
forty-
four,
eighty-
five,
one
hundred
and
eighty-
six, two
hundred
and
fifty
seven,
eighty-
one,
one

hundred
and
seventy
-nine,
two
hundred
and
two,
one
hundred
and
fifty
one,
one
hundred
and
eighty-
five,
three
hundred
and
eighty,
two
hundred
and six,
fifty.

One
hundred
and
sixty-
six,
eighty-
five,
two
hundred
and
ninety-
six,
seventy
-three,
one
hundred
and
seventy
-nine.

Two
hundred
and
twenty-
four,
two

hundred
and
fifty
six, two
hundred
and
eighty-
eight,
three
hundred
and
twenty-
eight,
one
hundred
and six.

Forty-six.

One hundred and
ninety-three.
seventy-one, nine,
fifty-four, one
hundred and
ninety-four.

The Abyss Yawns

?Tyger? ?Tyger? [1]

, ,

;

,

?

．
?
?
, ?
, ,
?
,
? ?

93

?   ,

      ?

?   ,

‘   :

?

?

,

:

,

?

; , " : ; , . "

" : ,,,, . "

" ; ' , ' . "

" ; ; ' ' . "

" ; , . "

" , .. "

— ' ! , , ; , .

Youth and Age ³

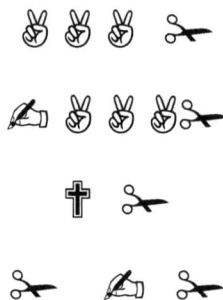

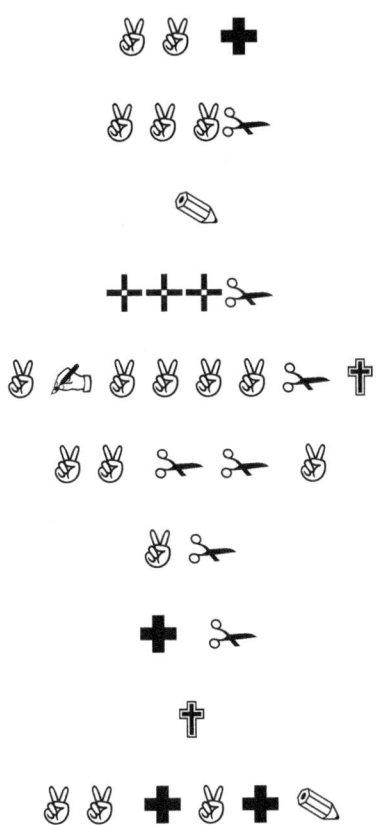

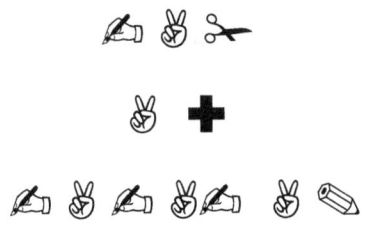

Seeing the Nighttingale [4]

,,,

, - :

'
,, ——

,⁻ ,,,

!

' - , - ,,, •

,,,⁻;

,,°

,,,,,,,

,,, – ;

– ;

, ·

! !

,,, :

!

, – , ’ ; ·

,,,,,, – ;

, ;

– ’ ;

– ’ – , , .

. ’ .
,, ,,

, , !

, ——

.

, !

;

: ,,,, ;

'
     , , .

! ! ! .

! !

, , - ; ' : , ?

: — ?

Emily Dashing [5]

—

—

— —

— !

— —

— — —

— — —

— —

— —

— —

— — !

Stein's Buttons [6]

·

·

·

·

·

·

, ·

·

·

·

· ·

,

,

105

·

,

·   ·

·   ·

·

Stevens' Morphed [7]

,   ,   ,

,   ,

– –   . . . .

•

–   '   •

, , ,

– – •

•

•

•

,

- - .

Pounding Concrete [8]

     '
   '   '
     '
     '
     '
     '
  '   ' '
   ' '
    '   .
  ' ' '
    '
    '
   – '
   –
    '
    .
    '
    .
   ' '

–   ;

,

,   .

'   –   ;

,

, ,

, –   .

,

, ,

,   ;

, ,

,   ,

, ,

;   ,

,   ;

,   ;

,   ,

,   ;

,

,

.

,   ,

,   ,

,

,,   .

.   :

"   ,   ?

"   '   ,   ?"

:

"   . '

.   .

"

,

"

,

"   -,   .

"

, , , ,

"   .

,

"   "

.

, , ,

, , :

" ? ? ,

" ?

" ,

" . "

,

, : "

"

, ,

" . " .

. , ,

, , .

,

.

,

' , , ,

, , ,

,

. :

Pounding Too [9]

                 .

    ;   ;

          ,

    '   ' .

        ;

        .

      ,   ;

.

'

;

'   .

;

;

,

,

,   '

'

.

'
   .

'   ,

,
'

'

;   '

;

.   .   .

;   .

,

,

.

;   .

.

;   ;

:

;

;   ;

;

;

,
.
;
-
:

1887—1968 XXXX[10]

·

"　　　　　　" ：

"　　　　　　'　　" "

"（　）·

—'　·—

·

------- ≡ ------

117

Dot, Dot, Dot Duchamp[11]

. . . .

. . . .

. . . .

,   -

. . . .

. . . .

.   -

. . . .

. . . .

. . . .

. . . .

. . . .

-

. . . .

118

．．．．．．．．

．．．．．．．．．．．．．

．．．．．

．．．．．．．．．．．．．．．．

．．．．．．．．．．．．．．．．

．．．．．．．．．．．．．．．．

．．．．．．．．．．．．．．．．

．．．．．．．．．．．

．．．．．．．．．．．．．．．．

．．．．．．．

．．．．．．．．．．．．．．

，

．．．．．．．．．．．

．．．．．．．．．．．．．．．

．．．．．．．．．．．．．．．

．．．．．．．．．．．．．．．

119

. . . .

. . . .

!

. . . .

. . . .

Coming [12]

$$(\quad - \quad)$$

$$-$$

$$(\quad)$$

$$(\quad)$$

Walking O'Hara

1-5

6
'
7-10

11.
12-13

14.
'
15-21

'
22.
23-24

'
25.
26-33

1   William Blake, "Tyger…" Peter Ackroyd, *Blake, A Biography*, 1995.

2   William Wordsworth, #179, *Pelgrave*.

3   Samuel T. Coleridge, "Youth and Age" #289, *Pelgrave*.

4   John Keats, "Ode to a Nighttingale"# 244, *Pelgrave*.

5   Emily Dickinson, #187, edited by Thomas Johnson.

6   Gertrude Stein, "Susie Asado," *The Norton Anthology of Modern Poetry*, ed., edited by Richard Ellmann and Robert O'Clar.

7   Wallace Stevens, "Metamorphosis," *The Collected Poems of Wallace Stevens*, 1990.

8   Ezra Pound, "Canto One," *Poems for the Millenium, volume 1*, edited by Jerome Rothenberg and Pierre Joris.

9   Ezra Pound, "Canto 51," *Poems for the Millenium, volume 1*, edited by Jerome Rothenberg and Pierre Joris.

10

11   Marcel Duchamp, "SURcenSURE, *Poems for the Millenium, volume 1*, edited by Jerome Rothenberg and Pierre Joris.

12   e.e. cummings, #47, *50 Poems*, 1940.

13   The numbers are mine to designate lines.
Frank O'Hara, "Walking," *The Collected Poems of Frank O'Hara*.

HOLLY CRAWFORD

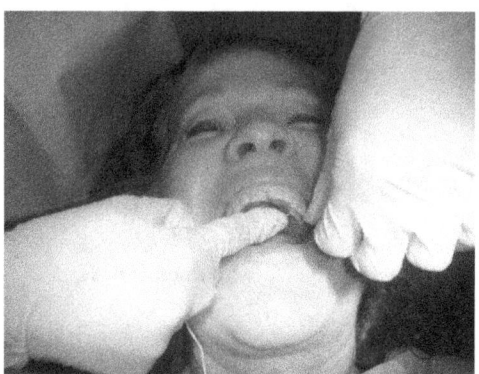

Holly Crawford, Ph.D., Director, of AC Institute, is a cross media artist, behavioral scientist, economist and art historian. Her art and poetry give new meanings and draws categories themselves into question through transformative juxtapositions. She examines mass media and pop culture and its relationship to art.

She has exhibited internationally. *13 Ways of Looking at a Blackbird* site specific installations in Florence, Valencia, Berlin, London, New York City and Southern California. *Offerings* project was a participating .net project at Ars Electronica and *Found Punctuation* was screened at the Tate Modern in 2007. Poetry performances at Beyond Baroque, Bowery Poetry Club and Lakeside Theatre Univesity Essex. Sound Art Limo and Critical Conversations in a Limo were part of Melbourne International Arts Festival in 2007.

She has written and edited books and papers that include: *Attached to the Mouse*, 2006, catalogue essay, "Disney and Pop" in *Once Upon a Time Walt Disney Studio, 2006, Artistic Bedfellows*, 2008, and Who Gets to Play? in *Popular Culture Values and the Arts,* 2009, edited by Ray B. Browne.

124

She received her Ph.D. from the University of Essex in Art History and Theory, B.A and M.A. in Economics and M.S. in Behavioral Science from UCLA. From 2004-2006, she was a non-clinical Fellow at NYU Medical School Psychanalytic Center. She has taught at UCLA in the Art Department and SVA. She founded and is the director of AC Institute, a non-profit space for experimental work in NYC (Chelsea).She is President of the American Friends of the University of Essex. She was born in California and now lives in New York City.

www.ingramcontent.com/pod-product-compliance
Lightning Source LLC
Chambersburg PA
CBHW081002170526
45158CB00010B/2875